CHIEFS & WARRIORS

NATIVE

NATIONS

VOLUME I

EDWARD S. CURTIS

CHIEFS
& WARRIORS

Christopher Cardozo

PRODUCED BY CALLAWAY EDITIONS

First Edition

(COVER)
SHOT IN THE HAND – APSAROKE, 1908

(FRONTISPIECE)
JACK RED CLOUD – OGALALA, 1907

ISBN 0-8212-2341-0

Library of Congress Catalog Card Number 96-76439

Bulfinch Press is an imprint and trademark of Little, Brown and Company (Inc.)
Published simultaneously in Canada by Little, Brown & Company (Canada) Limited

PRINTED IN HONG KONG

TABLE OF CONTENTS

PREFACE

The romance and beauty of a way of life unencumbered by the burdens of modern white "civilization" fascinated photographer/ethnographer Edward Sheriff Curtis. Curtis's thirty-year-long study of the native nations of the United States, Canada, and Alaska, which began in the 1890s, resulted in publication of The North American Indian, *twenty volumes and portfolios containing thousands of photographs and accompanying text on more than eighty tribal groups. During the process of recording visual and written information about Native American life and history, it is clear that Curtis was especially interested in tribal leaders and warriors, particularly those of the Northern Plains.*

Portraits of sitting chiefs and other leaders are found in nearly every volume of The North American Indian. *Most of these images capture the personality and character of the sitter in a way in which few photographers, if any, were able to, while others seem more oriented toward the presentation of a style of garment, a type of headdress, a ritual costume, or a typical battle tool or ceremonial object. In many cases, Curtis also carefully recorded the extensive life histories of the individuals he photographed, tracing their development and the achievements which eventually led to their recognition as prominent members of a tribe. This information is found in biographical sketches in the text portions of the various volumes.*

During the course of Curtis's three decades of travel and work throughout the western half of the North American continent, he came to have a special affinity for these men, and cultivated close relationships with some of the native nations' most important leaders. Curtis became close with Geronimo, Red Cloud, and Chief Joseph (to the point that he played a role in the funeral, burial, and other ceremonies surrounding Chief Joseph's death), among others.

The brave and heroic exploits of warriors, too, were preserved for posterity in Curtis's texts and photographs. Some of his photographs carry more general titles — The Scout, Ready for the Charge, The Chief, for instance — and, in many cases, are similar to so-called history paintings. They feature a warrior or chief figure or figures against the backdrop of a dramatic sky or an unspoiled landscape, preparing to do battle, on the hunt, congregating on horseback in full battle or ceremonial regalia. These images can be looked at as emotionally stirring symbolic portrayals of rapidly disappearing peoples or as idyllic, picturesque photographs that present a more idealized version of history.

Curtis's portraits of individual warriors often present men with serious expressions that communicate pride, wisdom, and experience. Reflective of Curtis's original work, the photographs of warriors selected herein are, in most cases, from the tribes of the Northern Plains region. The warrior and his activities were a very central aspect of Plains culture. These Plains tribes relied on hunting, requiring large areas of land on which to move freely in pursuit of game. Protecting that land, from other tribes and from the encroaching white man, was an imperative for tribal survival. — C.C.

BULL CHIEF – APSAROKE, 1908

Born 1825. Mountain Crow. Believing he could win success without fasting, he joined many war-parties, but always returned without honor. He therefore climbed Clouds Peak, the highest point in the Bighorn mountains, and there on the bare rocks he stood a day and a night. The mountain-rats ate holes in his robe and a fierce blizzard swept across the peak, so that he could not remain longer. Soon afterward the camp was moved, and he fasted four days and four nights in the southern part of Wolf mountains; no vision appeared. At this time all the men were possessed of an especial desire to count coups, and everybody was fasting. Bull Chief soon endured two more unsuccessful fasts, and then at the head of Redlodge creek, lance in hand and clad only in loin-cloth, moccasins, robe, and a piece of old lodge-cover, he fasted four days and four nights, much of the time in blinding snow. He saw his own lodge and a splendid bay horse standing in front of it. This vision was soon followed by the capture of a tethered bay, his first honor. Thenceforward he very frequently counted coup. . . . Married fifteen times; gave up thirteen of his wives. Father of thirteen children. Volume IV, pages 197-198.

THE SCOUT – NEZ PERCÉ, 1910

About two months were consumed in the journey to the buffalo country, and the nights were already growing cold. Although scouts were kept constantly in advance, the party came into sight of the first great herd while the whole cavalcade was in motion. The chiefs at once ordering the women and children to remain in the rear while the killing was in progress, the men quickly secured their "buffalo horses" and were ready for the slaughter. It was a great hunt, beginning before noon and lasting until night-fall. . . . For six days the hunting party remained in this place, feasting on the choicest parts of the buffalo-meat, and drying the remainder. Then for eight days they circled about in search of the main herd. The scouts, who were everywhere on the alert, reported many buffalo near the lake northwest of where Billings, Montana, now is, and the party went into camp on a small creek forming its outlet. In the morning the chiefs cried out: "To-day we will have a great hunt! The buffalo are thick all about us! The prairie is black with them!" Volume VIII, page 46.

(OPPOSITE)

FLATHEAD WARRIOR, 1910

The subject of the picture . . . is Black-tail Hawk, commonly called Pierre Lamoose, a descendant of the Iroquois Ignace La Mousse. His mother was a Flathead, his father half Kalispel and half Iroquois. Volume VII, page 46.

(OVERLEAF)

ATSINA WARRIORS, 1908

The Atsina, commonly designated Gros Ventres of the Prairie, are of the Algonquian stock and a branch of the Arapaho. . . .

The Atsina have been mentioned comparatively little in history, partly, no doubt, because of their isolation and of their indisposition to show the same hostility toward advancing civilization as their neighbors. . . . Yet the record of their tribal wars shows no indication of deficiency in courage or vigor. . . .

Men wore shirts and leggings of deerskin or antelope-skin, moccasins of buffalo-skin, and loin-cloth of old soft lodge-cover. The shirt was not sewn along the sides and under the arms, but only tied at intervals with cords. Like the leggings, it was frequently ornamented with dyed porcupine-quills. The hair was roached in front, and a braid hung at each temple. The single long braid at the back was usually spotted with orange paint. Warriors entering battle tied the hair in a mass on the top of the head. Volume V, pages 103, 111, 152.

(ABOVE)

A CHIEF OF THE DESERT –
NAVAHO, 1904

*Picturing not only the individual but a characteristic member of the
tribe – disdainful, energetic, self-reliant.* Folio plate 26, Volume I.

(OPPOSITE)

CHIEF GARFIELD – JICARILLA, 1904

*Some years ago the Jicarillas were all officially given Spanish or
English names. Many of them expressed a preference. This old man,
who was head-chief of the tribe at the time, selected the designation
Garfield.* Folio plate 21, Volume I.

COWICHAN WARRIOR, 1912

The word Kawútsun refers to a certain projecting rock on the side of the mountain Tsohélim, which guards the entrance of Cowichan river on the southeast coast of Vancouver island. Anglicized into Cowichan, the name appears frequently on the map, and is employed locally to designate the native inhabitants in the immediate vicinity of Cowichan harbor. Formerly these groups had no collective self-name, although they regarded themselves as closely related. They differed a little from the Nanaimo bands in the north and the numerous people of the Fraser river delta on the opposite mainland; yet these all formed a well-defined dialectic group, and ethnologists have agreed to let the term Cowichan include the tribes of Vancouver island between Nanoose bay and Saanich inlet, and the tribes of Fraser river from the coast to the mountain at Yale.

The Cowichan were more warlike than the average Salish tribe. With only the Comox intervening between them and Kwakiutl tribes, they not only were influenced by the northern culture but perforce they imbibed something of the ferocity of those savage head-hunters. Volume IX, page 32.

IRON BREAST – PIEGAN, 1900

The picture illustrates the costume of a member of the Bulls . . . an age society for many years obsolete. Folio plate 206, Volume VI.

The society of Bulls . . . an independent company of old men banded together . . . formed, probably about 1820, by a man who, in a dream in the mountains, saw a certain kind of dance, and on his return made the necessary insignia, sold it to a number of old men, and instructed them in the songs and dance. Some of the members had war-bonnets consisting of a circlet of feathers, others had circlet and trailer (the trailer representing the hump of the buffalo), and others caps formed of the scalp of the buffalo with the horns, shortened by cutting off the base, still attached. All wore buffalo-robes with the hairy side exposed. Volume VI, pages 27-28.

WEASEL TAIL – PIEGAN, 1900

The accoutrement of this brave . . . comprises the well-known war-bonnet of eagle-feathers and weasel-skins, deerskin shirt, bone necklace, grizzly-bear claw necklace, and tomahawk-pipe of Hudson's Bay Company origin. Folio plate 203, Volume VI.

START OF A WAR-PARTY, 1907

The political organization of the Teton Sioux could not be termed a confederacy. There were seven tribes composing this subfamily — the Ogalala, Brulés, Miniconjou, Sans Arcs, Two Kettles, Blackfeet (Sihasapa), and Hunkpapa — and each comprised several smaller groups or bands. Each tribe had a head-chief, wichásha-yátapika, *and usually each smaller unit a sub-chief,* itácha.

In serious warfare these several tribes were apt to form a close alliance for greater strength. . . . Generally, at the inception of a hostile movement of importance, a man of recognized leadership would take the initiative by organizing a war-party, and those who felt so disposed would join him. A notable instance is their last great war, which terminated in the victory of the Sioux and their allies over the troops at the battle of the Little Bighorn in 1876. Five of the Teton tribes were strongly represented: the Ogalala, Sans Arcs, Brulés, Miniconjou, and Hunkpapa, and these united Sioux tribes were aided by a large party of Cheyenne, while individual members of the other two Teton tribes also joined the hostile forces. Volume III, page XII.

THE OLD CHEYENNE, 1927

The Cheyenne wore clothing common to the tribes of the plains: for men, hip-leggings of deer- or buffalo-skin (for which in recent times cloth has been substituted); breech-cloth; moccasins of deer-, elk-, or buffalo-skin with rawhide soles. Volume XIX, page 224.

BLACK EAGLE – ASSINIBOIN, 1908

Born in 1834 on the Missouri below Williston, North Dakota. He was only thirteen years of age when he first went to war, and on this and on the next two occasions he gained no honors. On his fourth war excursion he was more successful, alone capturing six horses of the Yanktonai. While engaged in a fight with the Atsina near Fort Belknap, Montana, he killed a man and a boy. In a battle with Yanktonai he killed one of the enemy, and in another repeated the former success. Black Eagle led war-parties three times. He had a vision in which it was revealed to him that he would capture horses, and the vision was fulfilled. He had the same experience before he killed the man and the boy. He claims no medicine. Black Eagle married at the age of eighteen. Volume III, pages 182-183.

THE SCOUT – APACHE, 1906

The primitive Apache in his mountain home. Folio plate 13, Volume I.

AN OASIS IN THE BAD LANDS, 1905

This picture was made in the heart of the Bad Lands of South Dakota. The subject is the sub-chief Red Hawk. . . . Folio plate 80, Volume III.

Red Hawk . . . ("Scarlet Hawk"). Ogalala. Born 1854. First war-party in 1865 under Crazy Horse, against troops. Led an unsuccessful war-party at twenty-two against Shoshoni. First coup when twelve horse-raiding Blackfeet were discovered in a creek bottom and annihilated. Led another party against Shoshoni, but failed to find them; encountered and surrounded a white-horse troop. From a hill overlooking the fight Red Hawk saw soldiers dismount and charge. The Lakota fled, leaving him alone. A soldier came close and fired, but missed. Red Hawk did likewise, but while the soldier was reloading his carbine he fired again with his Winchester and heard a thump and "O-h-h-h!" A Cheyenne boy on horseback rushed in and struck the soldier, counting coup. Engaged in twenty battles, many with troops, among them the Custer fight of 1876; others with Pawnee, Apsaroke, Shoshoni, Cheyenne, and even with Sioux scouts. Volume III, page 188.

RAVEN BLANKET – NEZ PERCÉ, 1910

The territory of the Nez Percés was bounded on the east by the Bitterroot mountains of Idaho and Montana; on the south by the divide between Salmon river and Snake river, and, in Oregon, by the Powder River mountains; on the west by the Blue Mountains in Oregon, and, in Washington, by Tucanon creek from its source in the Blue mountains to its confluence with Snake river; on the north by the low divide between Snake river and the Palouse in Washington, and, in Idaho, by the range separating the headwaters of the Palouse from the tributaries of the Clearwater. . . .

The Nez Percés were a loosely associated group of local bands, each possessing its own territory and its own chief. It is true that they had a collective name for these bands, and that there were occasions when perhaps the greater part were in one camp, as at the camas meadows or during the fall fishing in the Wallowa and the Salmon. Nevertheless there was in reality no tribal organization. The bands were kindred, spoke the same language, and associated for mutual convenience and defence; but they remained distinct. The permanent villages were situated usually at the mouths of the tributaries of the larger rivers. Although each village community was independent of the others, and the head-chiefs of all such communities were theoretically of equal power, it was only natural that the influence of a man of unusual ability with a numerous following should extend itself beyond the borders of the band in which he was born. Volume VIII, pages 3-4.

GOOD LANCE – OGALALA, 1907

Born 1846. . . . He participated in ninety raids, mostly against the Pawnee. . . . From a famous Cheyenne medicine-man south of the Platte he bought medicine of pulverized roots tied in deerskin, as a charm against bullets and arrows. The medicine-man clothed him in a buffalo-robe with horns and tail attached, and rubbed the charm over his body. To prove that nothing could now harm him, the Cheyenne discharged a pistol at him, but the bullet inflicted only a skin wound in the arm; he then struck Good Lance in the back with a bayonet, but the resulting wound was slight. Good Lance paid the medicine-man a horse, and thereafter before entering a fight always rubbed the medicine over his body. Volume III, page 185.

HIGH HAWK, 1907

The subject is shown in all the finery of a warrior dressed for a gala occasion — scalp-shirt, leggings, moccasins, and pipe-bag, all embroidered with porcupine-quills; eagle-feather war-bonnet, and stone-headed war-club from the handle of which dangles a scalp. High Hawk is prominent among the Brulés mainly because he is now their leading historical authority, being much in demand to determine the dates of events important to his fellow tribesmen. Folio plate 87, Volume III.

THE LOOKOUT – APSAROKE, 1905

In stature and in vigor the Apsaroke, or Crows, excelled all other tribes of the Rocky Mountain region, and were surpassed by none in bravery and in devotion to the supernatural forces that gave them strength against their enemies. . . .

The country which the Apsaroke ranged and claimed as their own was an extensive one for so small a tribe. In area it may be compared, east and west, to the distance from Boston to Buffalo, and north to south, from Montreal to Washington — certainly a vast region to be dominated by a tribe never numbering more than fifteen hundred warriors. Volume IV, pages 3-4.

(OPPOSITE)

LONG FOX – ASSINIBOIN, 1908

Born in 1827 near Fort Berthold, North Dakota. He joined a war-party against the Mandan, capturing three horses. On another expedition against the same people he received an arrow wound. Subsequently, in an attack on the Assiniboin by the Sioux, he killed one, and in another fight with them he counted a first coup. The Assiniboin met a war-party of Piegan, and he captured one. Long Fox led against the Sioux a war-party that captured seven horses. He never had a vision. He married at thirty. Volume III, page 187.

(OVERLEAF)

THE PARLEY, 1908

The war-bonnet . . . could be worn only by men who had earned honors in war. When the young warrior had struck the necessary coups, he procured the needed eagle-feathers, took them with suitable presents to some one skilled in fashioning war-bonnets, and asked him to make a head-dress, that he might wear it as evidence of his bravery. Volume III, page 30.

CROW'S HEART – MANDAN, 1908

Each village had its head-chief, who held his position by reason of his surpassing all others as a warrior and a peacemaker. The office was therefore not hereditary. In the council, to which a man was admitted when he had sufficiently distinguished himself in battle, discussion was free, but the decision in the question at issue lay with the chief. He secured obedience to his commands through the military organization known as Black Mouths. Volume V, page 144.

PIEGAN WAR-BONNET AND COUP-STICK, 1909

War deeds of many kinds were recognized. The taking of a loaded gun from a man trying to shoot the aggressor was the bravest thing a warrior could do. Another great coup was to grapple with an unwounded enemy. Next came the charging alone against the enemy and striking one of them with a coup-stick. Striking a wounded man was an honor, but not the striking of a dead one, yet the taking of a weapon from a man, whether wounded or dead, was counted. Securing a horse in battle was a coup, and while the taking of horses from an enemy's camp was not a coup, it was an honor equal to capturing horses on the range. It was a coup for a man to lead a successful war-party, that is, one that killed an enemy or captured horses without the loss of a man. Volume VI, page 10.

BEAR BULL – BLACKFOOT, 1926

The plate illustrates an ancient Blackfoot method of arranging the hair.
Folio plate 640, Volume XVIII.

SINGING DEEDS OF VALOR, 1908

This most characteristic of the religious ceremonies of the Sioux was an occasion of thanksgiving, of propitiation, of supplication for divine power. Participation in the dance was entirely voluntary, a mental vow to worship the Mystery in this manner being expressed by a man ardently desiring the recovery of a sick relative; or surrounded by an enemy with escape apparently impossible; or, it might be, dying of hunger, with helpless children crying for food that he could not supply, since some inscrutable power had swept all game from forest and prairie. Others joined in the ceremony in the hope and firm belief that the Mystery, worshipped with such zeal and with such manifestation of valor would grant them successes against the enemy and consequent eminence at home; while always there was present the idea, perhaps subconscious, that the supernatural, even though a beneficent being, must be propitiated against future anger. Volume III, page 88.

CHIEF JOSEPH – NEZ PERCÉ, 1903

The name of Chief Joseph is better known than that of any other Northwestern Indian. To him popular opinion has given the credit of conducting a remarkable strategic movement from Idaho to northern Montana in the flight of the Nez Percés in 1877. . . . Their unfortunate effort to retain what was rightly their own makes an unparalleled story in the annals of the Indians' resistance to the greed of the whites. That they made this final effort is not surprising. Indeed, it is remarkable that so few tribes rose in a last struggle against such dishonest and relentless subjection. Folio plate 256, Volume VIII.

TWO WHISTLES – APSAROKE, 1908

Born 1856. Mountain Crow of the Not Mixed clan and Lumpwood organization. Never achieved a recognized coup, but at the age of eighteen he led a party consisting, besides himself, of two others, which captured a hundred horses from the Sioux. Participated in four severe battles against Arapaho and Sioux, one being the engagement at the mouth of Pryor creek. First fasted at the age of thirty-five. The first night he saw the war-bonnet of a Sioux; the next day he cut the skin and flesh of his arms in representation of eight hoof-prints; and that night the moon came to him and said, "At Íyehopish (the country about Livingston, Montana) are buffalo and horses mixed; you will never be poor." In the outbreak caused by the medicine-man Wraps Up His Tail, at Crow Agency in 1887, Two Whistles was shot in the arm and breast, necessitating the amputation of the arm above the elbow. His medicine of hawk was purchased with a horse from a Sioux. Volume IV, page 207.

MASSELOW, KALISPEL CHIEF, 1910

THE PEACE-OFFICER –
KALISPEL, 1910

The tribe now includes not more than a hundred persons, whose cabins here and there dot the valley on the eastern side of the river for a distance of some fifteen miles southward from Mission creek. Timothy planted by the priests more than sixty years ago has taken possession of broad meadows, which now yield the hay upon which the people depend almost wholly for their support. Each summer they leave their ill-ventilated cabins and pitch small lodges in a camp at the camas meadow opposite Cusick, Washington, where some semblance of their former life may yet be observed. The smoke curls upward from a dozen tipis. Women, old and young, are scattered over the fields plying their root-diggers and filling their baskets with camas bulbs. A bark canoe slips silently through the water toward the paddler's favorite fishing ground, and on the sloping grassy bank, among other upturned canoes, another boatman bends over his craft, deftly caulking its seams with spruce-gum. . . .

Their chief, Masselow (a corruption of the French name Marcellon), son of his predecessor, Victor, controls them more by the aid of tribal custom and the strong right arm of the peace officer, who at his command administers punishment with the lash. . . . They have never made a treaty with the Government, and have held their homes only by right of occupancy, but in 1909 steps were taken to grant them in severalty lands sufficient for their maintenance. Volume VII, page 53.

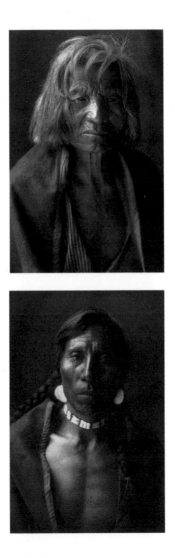

APSAROKE WAR-CHIEF, 1908

*The three fox-tails hanging from the coup-stick show the subject —
Medicine Crow . . . to be the possessor of three first coups, that is, in
three encounters he was the first to strike one of the enemy's force. The
necklace consists of beads, and the large ornaments at the shoulders are
abalone shells.* Folio plate 112, Volume IV.

*Born 1848. Mountain Crow; member of the Newly Made Lodge clan
and of the Lumpwood organization. At eighteen he fasted four
days and three nights, and on the morning of the fourth day a spirit
resembling a white man appeared and foretold the passing away of the
buffalo and the coming of many white men with cattle, horses, and
steamboats. His medicine of hawk was purchased from another man.
Counted three first coups, captured five guns and two tethered horses,
and led ten successful war-parties. In a fight with the Nez Percés he
killed a warrior, counted first coup upon him, and captured his gun —
two regular honors at one time, besides the distinction of killing an
enemy. This act he twice repeated in battles with the Arapaho and the
Sioux. Twice he fought on the side of the white men when "their flag
was on the ground": once against the Nez Percés in Chief Joseph's
retreat, and again under General Crook when the Sioux under
Sitting Bull were fleeing across the Canadian border. Medicine Crow
participated in ten severe fights, killed three men, had two horses shot
under him, and had the distinction of having "thrown away" six
wives.* Volume IV, page 203.

(OPPOSITE)

FOG IN THE MORNING –
APSAROKE, 1908

Born about 1858. Mountain Crow; Not Mixed clan; Lumpwood organization. Never won an honor. After the death of his son he fasted many times until at length he had a vision, after which he claimed "White Man Above" as his medicine, also Thunder. Thereafter he gained considerable property, and his success being attributed to his medicine, he derived some fame — and more property — as a dispenser of good luck. Volume IV, page 200.

(OVERLEAF)

THE CHIEF – KLAMATH, 1923

The subject of this plate, in deerskin suit and feathered war-bonnet of the Plains culture, is shown against a background of Crater lake and its precipitous rim towering a thousand feet above the water. Folio plate 470, Volume XIII.

BEAR'S BELLY – ARIKARA, 1908

Born in 1847 at Fort Clark, in the present North Dakota. . . . He became a member of the Bears in the medicine fraternity, and relates the following story of an occurrence connected with that event: "Needing a bear-skin in my medicine-making, I went . . . into the White Clay hills. . . . Coming suddenly to the brink of a cliff I saw below me three bears. . . . I wanted a bear, but to fight three was hard. I decided to try it, and, descending, crept up to within forty yards of them. . . . One bear was standing with his side toward me, another was walking slowly toward him on the other side. I waited until the second one was close to the first, and pulled the trigger. The farther one fell; the bullet had passed through the body of one and into the brain of the other. The wounded one charged, and I ran . . . then turned and shot again, breaking his backbone. . . . A noise caused me to remember the third bear, which I saw rushing upon me. . . . He rose on his hindlegs, and I shot, with my gun nearly touching his chest. . . . The bear with the broken back was dragging himself about with his forelegs, and I went to him and said, 'I came looking for you to be my friend, to be with me always.' Then I reloaded my gun and shot him through the head. His skin I kept, but the other two I sold. Volume V, page 178.

SLOW BULL – OGALALA, 1907

Born 1844. First war-party at fourteen, under Red Cloud, against Apsaroke. Engaged in fifty-five battles with Apsaroke, Shoshoni, Ute, Pawnee, Blackfeet, and Kutenai. Struck seven first coups. At seventeen he captured one hundred and seventy horses from Apsaroke. In the same year he received medicine from buffalo in a dream while he slept on a hilltop, not fasting, but resting from travel on the war-path. Counted two honors in one fight, when the Lakota charged an Apsaroke camp and were routed. Slow Bull returned to the enemy; his horse stepped into a hole and fell, and an Apsaroke leaped on him. He threw his antagonist off, jumped on his horse, and struck his enemy in the face with his bow. At that moment another Apsaroke dashed up and dealt him a glancing blow in the back with a hatchet. Slow Bull counted coup on him also. He had been a subchief of the Ogalala since 1878. Volume III, page 189.

A YOUNG NEZ PERCÉ, 1910

The Nez Percés are by other tribes given credit for a proud spirit which led them into deeds of great bravery. Their warfare being almost altogether with the Shoshoni and the Bannock, whose territory lay immediately south of theirs, and with the Piegan, Atsina, Sioux, and sometimes the Apsaroke, whom they encountered in the Montana plains, it was natural that their war customs were of the kind common to the plains. When a large party was being organized, the names of the leaders were publicly announced, and in the evening was held a dance called Pâhamn for the purpose of recruiting. Men who intended to participate in the campaign joined in the dance, and at the end of each song the names of the new recruits were called out. Small parties were organized without this procedure. On the evening before their departure the warriors, with perhaps a number of friends to assist in the singing, went from lodge to lodge with a dry, stiff rawhide on which they beat with switches, while singing their individual war-songs. Volume VIII, page 161.

CHEYENNE WARRIORS, 1905

In addition to their dances and their raids, the warrior societies performed the duties of the so-called soldiers common to all plains peoples. They were the camp police, and they preserved order on the general buffalo hunt. They enforced the orders of the chiefs. But more than that, their wishes were consulted before any matter of public interest was settled. They were in fact the real ruling power, the only body that could compel obedience. Volume VI, page 108.

THREE WHITE COWS – ATSINA, 1908

Born in 1854 near Milk river, Montana. His first war experience was had at the age of eighteen. He participated in the battle in which . . . twenty-one Piegan were killed . . . and won a second coup. His friend was killed in the thick of a battle with the Sioux, and the dead boy's father told Three White Cows to get his horse from the enemy, which he did, charging into the middle of the Piegan and leading the horse out. Later in this fight he went back and rescued an old man whose horse had become unmanageable. Volume V, page 184.

RED CLOUD – OGALALA, 1905

Born 1822. At the age of fifteen he accompanied a war-party which killed eighty Pawnee. . . . At seventeen he led a party that killed eight of the same tribe. During his career he killed two Shoshoni and ten Apsaroke. . . . Red Cloud received his name, in recognition of his bravery, from his father after the latter's death. Before that his name had been Two Arrows, Wa^n-n^{n}íti. His brother-in-law, Nachíli, gave him medicine tied up in a little deerskin bag. Always before going to war Red Cloud rubbed this over his body. All the tribe regarded his medicine as very potent. He first gained notice as a leader by his success at Fort Phil. Kearny in 1866, when he killed Captain Fetterman and eighty soldiers. In the following year he led a large party, two to three thousand, it is said, in an attack on a wood-train at the same post, but was repulsed with great loss. . . . Previously only chief of the Bad Face band of Ogalala, he became head-chief of the tribe after the abandonment of Fort Phil. Kearny. Red Cloud was prevented from joining in the Custer fight by the action of General Mackenzie in disarming him and his camp. Volume III, page 187.

GRAY BEAR – YANKTONAI, 1908

Born in South Dakota in 1845. When fourteen years of age he joined a war-party, but achieved no honors. He fought against the Hidatsa, running down, while mounted, a horseless warrior and counting first coup. In another raid against the Hidatsa he successfully captured nine tethered horses on a dark and stormy night. Gray Bear's tutelary deities were the sun and the horses he rode in battle. Volume III, page 186.

IN THE BAD LANDS, 1904

This striking picture was made at Sheep Mountain in the Bad Lands of Pine Ridge reservation, South Dakota. Folio plate 119, Volume III.

NIGHT SCOUT – NEZ PERCÉ, 1910

Constant foes of the Nez Percés were the Bannock, the Shoshoni, the Coeur d'Alênes, and the Spokan. With the Flatheads and Kalispel, the Yakima, the Columbia river people as far down as the Dalles, including the Umatilla, the Cayuse, and the Wallawalla, they were always at peace. On their journeys to the buffalo country they were often in conflict with different tribes met in the region traversed; but generally they were on friendly terms with the Apsaroke, such amity being almost a necessity, for on it depended their passage through the western gateway to the southern buffalo plains. Often the Nez Percés met Flatheads and other Indians from the east on the plains of Oyaíp, and there bartered with them for buffalo-robes and meat. They went also to the Columbia at the Dalles, where they reëxchanged their buffalo-robes for such articles as the river Indians possessed — pounded fish, wapato roots, shell beads. In rare instances men went to the mouth of the river, to return with stories of the great water and its monsters — whales, porpoises, and sea-lions. Volume VIII, page 49.

(ABOVE)

OLD PERSON – PIEGAN, 1911

The young men eagerly seize every occasion of public festivity to don the habiliments of their warrior fathers. Folio plate 204, Volume VI.

(OPPOSITE)

A PIEGAN WAR-BONNET, 1926

The Piegans though the same people as the Blackfeet and Bloods, imagine themselves to be a superior race, braver and more virtuous than their own countrymen, whom they always seem to despise for their vicious habits and treacherous conduct. They are proud and haughty. . . .

War seems to be the Piegans' sole delight; their discourse always turns upon that subject; one war-party no sooner arrives than another sets off. . . . Volume XVIII, pages 179-180.

SHOT IN THE HAND, 1908

Born about 1841. . . . By fasting he obtained his hawk-medicine; it was his custom to make a powder of a hawk's heart, sweet-grass, and green paint, and to eat a portion of the mixture just before going into battle. Counted three dákshe, *captured three guns and one tethered horse, but lacked the medicine to become a war-leader. Once rushed up a height to strike the Piegan who were entrenched on the summit, when a shot brought him to the ground; he arose and charged again, and was again shot, this time rolling to the foot of the hill. Seven times he struck an enemy who was firing at him. After the suspension of intertribal hostilities the Ogalala chief Red Cloud, who boasted of having performed this feat four times, sent a challenge to the Apsaroke to produce a man who could equal the record, and Shot In The Hand was promptly named. Shot In The Hand played a spectacular part in the battle against the Sioux on Pryor creek. . . . On another occasion he dismounted beside his father, who had been shot in the thigh, and though the latter was killed the son was rescued, wounded in the arm. Four times in as many different fights he seized an unharmed enemy by the hair and hurled him from his horse. . . . He "threw away" seven of his eight wives.* Volume IV, page 204.

STRUCK BY CROW – OGALALA, 1907

Born 1847. At eleven he accompanied a party against the Apsaroke, the one in which Fast Thunder served as a warrior. He participated in ten battles, most of them against the Apsaroke, and fought four times against troops, three of these occasions being the Fetterman massacre, the engagement with Crook's command at the Rosebud, and the battle of the Little Bighorn. Counted coup twice, both in the same fight, when twenty Flatheads and two Sioux were killed. Fasted four times in the Bighorn mountains and experienced a vision. Early in the morning he took five tanned buffalo-skins to the summit and gave them to the Mystery. He remained on his feet until long after darkness had fallen, and then as he lay half sleeping he saw the fork of a river, and beside it a ridge over which came many horses driven by a man. Some of the horses were white. The next day at sunset he returned to his camp and went into the sweat-lodge. A short time after this Struck By Crow accompanied a raiding party and captured some white horses. Volume III, page 189-190.

NEZ PERCÉ WARRIOR, 1905

The office of chief was hereditary, but not strictly so, since public opinion could cause the rejection of an unfit heir. The old men and the warriors constituted an advisory body which, if its opinion ran counter to that of the chief, was expected to yield if he stood firm. Volume VIII, page 160.

READY FOR THE CHARGE –
APSAROKE, 1908

*The picture shows well the old-time warrior with bow and arrow in
position, two extra shafts in his bow-hand, and a fourth between his
teeth ready for instant use.* Folio plate 125, Volume IV.

EAGLE ELK – OGALALA, 1907

Born 1853. At fourteen he went against the Apsaroke with a party which killed four near the Bighorn mountains. He participated in many battles against the Apsaroke, Shoshoni, Blackfeet, Cheyenne, Assiniboin, Omaha, and Ute, the severest being that with the Apsaroke and Nez Percés at the mouth of Arrow (Pryor) creek. Eagle Elk was then about twenty years of age, and thinks there were a thousand men on each side, the Sioux being aided by Cheyenne and Arapaho. The fight lasted from daylight until darkness, with neither side victorious. Each lost about ten killed and many wounded. Eagle Elk fought under Crazy Horse against General Miles at Tongue river, and under the same leader in the Custer fight. He fasted in the Black Hills four days and four nights, but had no vision, and never acquired any fighting medicine. Volume III, pages 183-184.

(OPPOSITE)

SPOTTED JACK-RABBIT –
APSAROKE, 1908

Born 1864. Mountain Crow; Never Shoots, Packs Game clan. Son of Shot In The Hand. At sixteen, having returned from his first war-party without accomplishing anything because a fall from his horse had broken his shoulder, he decided that he must gain power from the spirits by fasting. He went into the mountains, but received no vision. In all he fasted ten times, and at last was rewarded with a vision. He received no medicine from it, however, and was compelled to take that of his father. Spotted Jack-rabbit counted one dákshe, an unusual honor for a man born so near the close of intertribal hostilities. Scouted with Miles against the Bannock, and with Howard against the Nez Percés. Was shot through the leg in the threatened uprising at Crow Agency in 1887. Volume IV, pages 206-207.

(OVERLEAF)

THE CHIEF AND HIS STAFF –
APSAROKE, 1905

Among the Apsaroke the chiefs were not elected: a man had a recognized standing according to his deeds, and so definite was the system of honors that there was never doubt as to the proper successor to the head-chieftainship. Volume IV, page 9.

LIST OF PLATES

ACKNOWLEDGMENTS

I would like to acknowledge my profound personal and professional debt to Edward S. Curtis. Without his extraordinary vision, talents, and commitment, none of this would be possible. Having had the opportunity to be so intimately involved with his work has been one of the great joys of my adult life.

I would also like to express my sincere gratitude to the many wonderful individuals at Callaway Editions, Inc. Their commitment to bringing the work of Edward Curtis to the world involves much hard work. I particularly want to thank my patient and capable editor Robert Janjigian, as well as Nicholas Callaway, Richard Benson, True Sims, Jessica Allan, Jennifer Wagner, Daniel Benson, and the many others at Callaway Editions who played such important roles in making this book a reality.

I also wish to thank my assistant Angela Spann for her hard work and many contributions, and Darren Quintenz and Howard Gottlieb, whose faith in me and whose deep interest in the work of Edward Curtis have also been instrumental in making all of this possible. — C.C.

COLOPHON

Chiefs & Warriors was produced by Callaway Editions, Inc.
70 Bedford Street, New York, NY 10014.
Robert Janjigian, editor. Jennifer Wagner, designer.

Type was composed with Quark Xpress software for Macintosh using a redrawn Franklin Gothic Extra Condensed typeface and the Centaur typeface from Adobe Systems.

The images selected for this volume were reproduced from an archive of Edward S. Curtis photographs contained on a CD-ROM. Richard and Daniel Benson converted these RGB files to a single gray-scale file, from which four printing negatives were generated. These negatives were printed as quadratones with ink colors that replicate the hues found in Curtis's original photogravures.

Captions accompanying the Curtis images presented herein are excerpts from Curtis's original texts found in the twenty volumes and twenty portfolios of The North American Indian, published from 1907 to 1930, available on CD-ROM through Christopher Cardozo, Inc., 2419 Lake Place, Minneapolis, MN 55405.

The endpaper design was created using symbols originally printed on the title pages of volumes I, II, III, IV, V, VII, VIII, X, XII, XIII, XIV, XV, XVIII *and* XIX *of* The North American Indian.

This book was printed and bound by Palace Press International, Hong Kong, under the supervision of Raoul Goff.